GREEN BERETS

Simon Rose

MEDIA ENHANCED BOOKS

AV²
BY WEIGL™

ADDED VALUE • AUDIO VISUAL

www.av2books.com

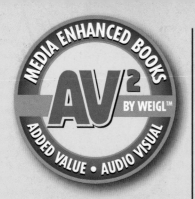

AV² provides enriched content that supplements and complements this book. Weigl's AV² books strive to create inspired learning and engage young minds in a total learning experience.

Your AV² Media Enhanced books come alive with...

 Audio
Listen to sections of the book read aloud.

 Key Words
Study vocabulary, and complete a matching word activity.

 Video
Watch informative video clips.

 Quizzes
Test your knowledge.

Go to **www.av2books.com,** and enter this book's unique code.

BOOK CODE

L948785

 Embedded Weblinks
Gain additional information for research.

 Slide Show
View images and captions, and prepare a presentation.

AV² by Weigl brings you media enhanced books that support active learning.

 Try This!
Complete activities and hands-on experiments.

... and much, much more!

Published by AV² by Weigl
350 5th Avenue, 59th Floor
New York, NY 10118
Website: www.av2books.com   www.weigl.com

Library of Congress Cataloging-in-Publication Data
Rose, Simon, 1961-
  Green Berets / Simon Rose.
     p. cm. -- (U.S. Armed Forces)
 Audience: Grades 4-6.
 Includes index.
 ISBN 978-1-62127-451-3 (hbk. : alk. paper) -- ISBN 978-1-62127-457-5 (pbk. : alk. paper)
 1. United States. Army. Special Forces--Juvenile literature. I. Title.
 UA34.S64R68 2014
 356'.16--dc23
                          2012040453

Printed in the United States of America in North Mankato, Minnesota
1 2 3 4 5 6 7 8 9   17 16 15 14 13

022013
WEP301112

Project Coordinator: Aaron Carr
Designer: Mandy Christiansen

Photo Credits
The photos used in this book are model-released stock images. They are meant to serve as accurate representations of U.S. Special Operations personnel, even though the people in the photos may not be special operators. Weigl acknowledges Getty Images, iStockphoto, Dreamstime, Alamy, and the U.S. Department of Defense as the primary image suppliers for this book.

Every reasonable effort has been made to trace ownership and to obtain permission to reprint copyright material. The publisher would be pleased to have any errors or omissions brought to their attention so that they may be corrected in subsequent printings.

CONTENTS

WHAT ARE THE GREEN BERETS?

The United States Army Special Forces, also known as the Green Berets, is a division of the U.S. Army that takes part in especially dangerous missions. Green Berets carry out most of their operations on land, but they also may use helicopters or other aircraft and ships on missions.

The Special Forces is one of the two main Army groups under the Army Special Operations Command (ASOC). The other main ASOC group is the 75th Ranger Regiment, also known as the Rangers. ASOC is part of the United States Special Operations Command (USSOCOM). The Department of Defense is in charge of USSOCOM and all branches of the Armed Forces except the Coast Guard. The Green Berets have about 5,500 members on active duty. There are also more than 1,000 Green Berets in the Army **National Guard** who may be called to active duty when needed.

★ Green Berets operate in small teams of 12 men. Each man is a specialist in a specific skill.

USSOCOM Organizational Structure

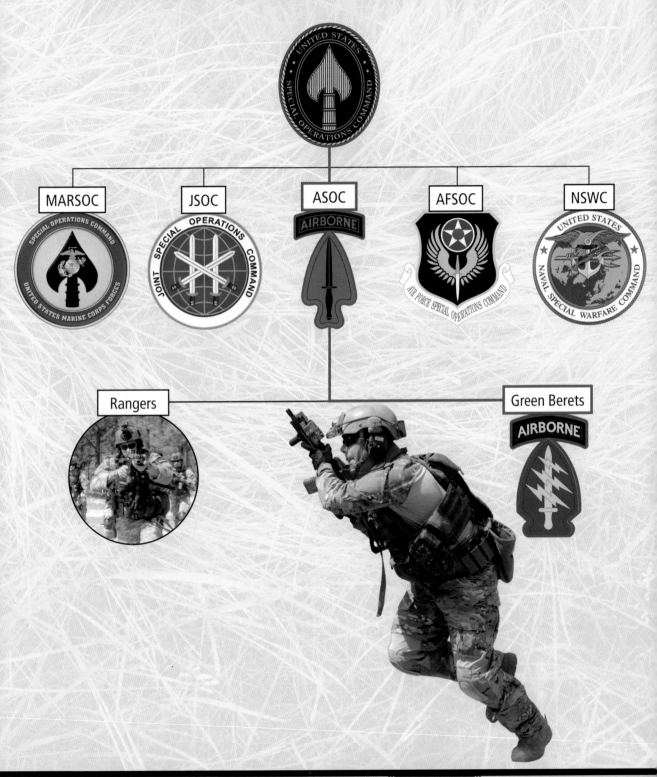

MARSOC

JSOC

ASOC

AFSOC

NSWC

Rangers

Green Berets

PROTECTING THE COUNTRY

The Green Berets defend the United States and protect its activities and interests around the world. They work with other U.S. Army units and other branches of the Armed Forces in times of war. During peacetime, they are always prepared to take action wherever they are needed.

The U.S. Special Forces are divided into five active-duty groups and two National Guard groups. Each group is responsible for Special Forces operations in a certain part of the world. Green Berets are trained in the languages and cultures within their region of responsibility. In recent years, Green Berets from all groups have worked outside their specified area, mainly in Iraq and Afghanistan.

On the Front Lines

On the battlefield, Green Berets are involved in operations on the ground. They take part in unconventional warfare, such as secret missions behind enemy lines, **guerilla warfare, reconnaissance,** rescuing **hostages**, and fighting **terrorism**. Their missions often prepare the way for larger attacks by the Army. When the fighting is over, Green Berets may stay and help the country maintain order and train local armed forces.

THE GREEN BERET MOTTO

De Oppresso Liber is the motto of the Green Berets. It is supposed to be a Latin phrase that translates into English as "To Free From Oppression." The words are not grammatically correct, but the motto has been used for many years. It has become part of the Green Beret tradition.

HISTORY OF THE GREEN BERETS

The United States Army Special Forces was formed in 1952. Its mission at the time was to help defend Western Europe against invasion by the Soviet Union and its allies. Over time, the Army Special Forces became better known as the Green Berets.

1952
★ The U. S. Special Forces is formed

1965 TO 1973
★ Vietnam War

1980s
★ Special Forces personnel train El Salvador soldiers to fight against communist rebels

1961
★ Special Forces personnel act as advisors to soldiers in Laos and Vietnam in Southeast Asia

1970
★ Green Berets attempt to rescue American prisoners of war (POWs) in North Vietnam

1965

1983

The Green Berets have been involved in military operations throughout the world. They have carried out missions in Europe, Asia, and South America. In Vietnam and El Salvador, they fought in the jungle. In Iraq and Afghanistan, they fought in the desert.

1989
★ Green Berets take part in the invasion of Panama

2001
★ The U.S. Army leads the invasion of Afghanistan

1991
★ Persian Gulf War

2003
★ The U.S. Army leads the invasion of Iraq

LATE 1980s
★ Special Forces soldiers fight **drug trafficking** and terrorism in Columbia

1991

2001

GREEN BERET BASES AROUND THE WORLD

Green Berets work closely with the Army and other branches of the U.S. military, sometimes even using the same bases. This is true both in the United States and throughout the world.

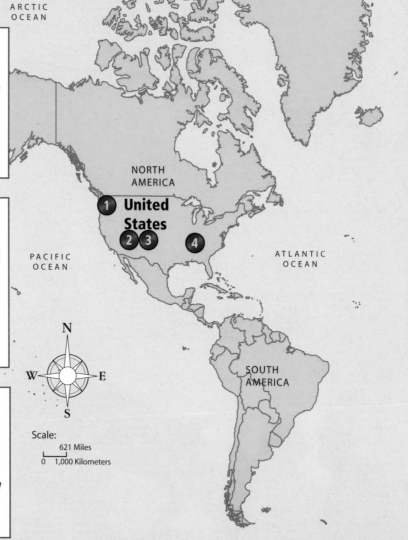

1 Washington

Joint Base Lewis-McChord near Tacoma is home to the 1st Special Forces Group. Green Berets in this group are mainly responsible for the Pacific Ocean region.

2 Utah

The 19th Special Forces Group is headquartered in Draper. This group is responsible for Green Beret operations in Europe and Western and Southeast Asia.

3 Colorado

Fort Carson near Colorado Springs is the home of the 10th Special Forces Group. Members of this group mostly work in Europe, Turkey, Israel, Lebanon, and North Africa.

ARCTIC OCEAN

NORTH AMERICA

1 United States

2 3 **4**

PACIFIC OCEAN

ATLANTIC OCEAN

SOUTH AMERICA

Scale:
621 Miles
0   1,000 Kilometers

N
W   E
S

SOUTHERN OCEAN

④ Kentucky
Fort Campbell is the main base of the 5th Special Forces Group. These Green Berets work mainly in the Middle East and North Africa.

⑤ Germany
Some Green Berets from the 10th Special Forces Group are based at Patch Barracks in Stuttgart, Germany. This base is the headquarters of Special Operations Command Europe.

ARCTIC OCEAN

ASIA

EUROPE

⑤

PACIFIC OCEAN

⑥

⑥ Japan
Some Green Berets from the 1st Special Forces Group are based at the Torii Station U.S. Army base in Okinawa, Japan.

AFRICA

INDIAN OCEAN

AUSTRALIA

Green Beret Uniforms

THE GREEN BERET

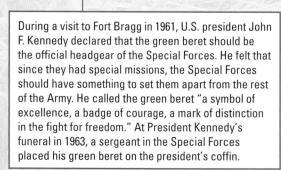

During a visit to Fort Bragg in 1961, U.S. president John F. Kennedy declared that the green beret should be the official headgear of the Special Forces. He felt that since they had special missions, the Special Forces should have something to set them apart from the rest of the Army. He called the green beret "a symbol of excellence, a badge of courage, a mark of distinction in the fight for freedom." At President Kennedy's funeral in 1963, a sergeant in the Special Forces placed his green beret on the president's coffin.

Green Berets work on secret missions behind enemy lines. Instead of wearing uniforms, they often dress like local people in order to fit in. The Geneva Convention is an international treaty that protects soldiers who are captured during wartime. Soldiers not wearing uniforms do not have this protection. Green Berets working in secret may be tortured or killed if captured by the enemy, making their job even more dangerous.

ARMY COMBAT UNIFORM

If working closely with the Army on a mission, Green Berets may wear the Army Combat Uniform. This uniform is designed in the Universal Camouflage Pattern. The pattern blends tan, gray, and green to make soldiers harder to see in the desert, the woods, and other places. The Improved Outer Tactical Vest, or IOTV body armor, can be worn over the jacket.

The helmet is made from material known as Kevlar or Twaron. Goggles protect the eyes. A night-vision device can be attached to the helmet for operations at night or in low-light conditions.

The trousers are worn with a 2-inch (5-centimeter) wide nylon belt. They have two storage pockets at the thighs and two pockets at the calves. Soldiers wear tan-colored combat boots. They also use elbow pads, kneepads, and gloves.

GREEN BERET WEAPONS

The Green Berets use some of the same weapons as other special operations forces in the U.S. Armed Forces.

M4 RIFLE

The M4 carbine rifle is one of the main guns used by the Green Berets. The M4 operates on gas and can be fired in **semiautomatic** or in bursts of three rounds. Its barrel is 14.5 inches (37 centimeters) long. The shorter barrel allows the soldiers to better use the rifle in tight spaces.

M9 BERETTA PISTOL

The M9 Beretta is a semiautomatic pistol. It is one of the standard handguns used by the U.S. military. The pistol has a 4.7-inch (12-cm) long barrel and a **magazine** containing 15 rounds. The M9 can be fitted with lights, lasers, and other accessories.

M136 ROCKET LAUNCHER

The M136 is a lightweight, one-shot rocket launcher fired from the shoulder. The projectile has fins to make it fly straighter. The rocket launcher can be fitted with different **warheads.** The High Explosive Dual Purpose (HEDP) warhead is mostly used against bunkers and buildings. After the weapon is fired, it can be thrown away.

M67 GRENADE

The M67 grenade weighs 14 ounces (397 grams) and has a safety clip to prevent it from exploding accidentally. A soldier can throw the grenade about 100 to 115 feet (30 to 35 meters). The M67 explodes in 4 to 5.5 seconds after the safety clip is pulled. Steel fragments from the grenade can seriously injure a person within 45 feet (14 meters) of the explosion. A person within 15 feet (5 m) can be killed.

MK12 SPECIAL PURPOSE RIFLE

The MK12 is a compact and lightweight weapon used by Green Beret **snipers**. It is a semiautomatic version of the M16, a similar gun used by other members of the Armed Forces. It has a magazine that contains either 20 or 30 rounds of ammunition. The weapon has a range of 600 yards (549 m). It can be fitted with different attachments, such as scopes and infrared and laser sights.

MP5 SUBMACHINE GUN

The MP5 is a lightweight, compact submachine gun that is fired from the shoulder or hip. It has an 8.9-inch (23-cm) long barrel and can fire 800 rounds per minute. The weapon's accuracy and reliability have made it a favorite of military forces in many countries.

JOINING THE GREEN BERETS

Anyone wishing to join the Green Berets must be a male U.S. citizen or permanent resident. People must be between 20 and 30 years of age, have a high school education, and be in good physical condition. They must also have excellent vision. To qualify for **officer** training programs, applicants must have a college degree. Women are not allowed to join the Green Berets.

Applying to the Green Berets

Civilians can apply to become Green Berets before joining the Army.

Step One: Apply online or talk to a recruiter and submit your application in person

Step Two: Achieve a high score on the Armed Services Vocational Aptitude Battery (ASVAB)

Step Three: Qualify for a **security clearance**

Step Four: Qualify and volunteer for airborne training

Step Five: Achieve a high score in the Army Physical Fitness Test

Step Six: Successfully complete the Pre-Basic Training Task List

Boot Camp

Basic training for Army recruits is often called Boot Camp, which takes 10 weeks. Green Beret trainees must meet the physical fitness requirements of the Special Forces Assessment and Selection (SFAS) course, which lasts three weeks. The course involves physical training and measures leadership and teamwork.

OATH OF ENLISTMENT

❝I do solemnly swear that I will support and defend the Constitution of the United States against all enemies, foreign and domestic; that I will bear true faith and allegiance to the same; and that I will obey the orders of the President of the United States and the orders of the officers appointed over me, according to regulations and the Uniform Code of Military Justice. So help me God.❞

The next step is the Special Forces Qualification Course (SFQC), or Q Course. This course can take from six months to a year to complete, and includes training in unconventional warfare, survival skills, and foreign languages. After successfully completing this course, Special Forces soldiers are then eligible for many advanced courses. These include training as parachutists, divers, snipers, and other specialists.

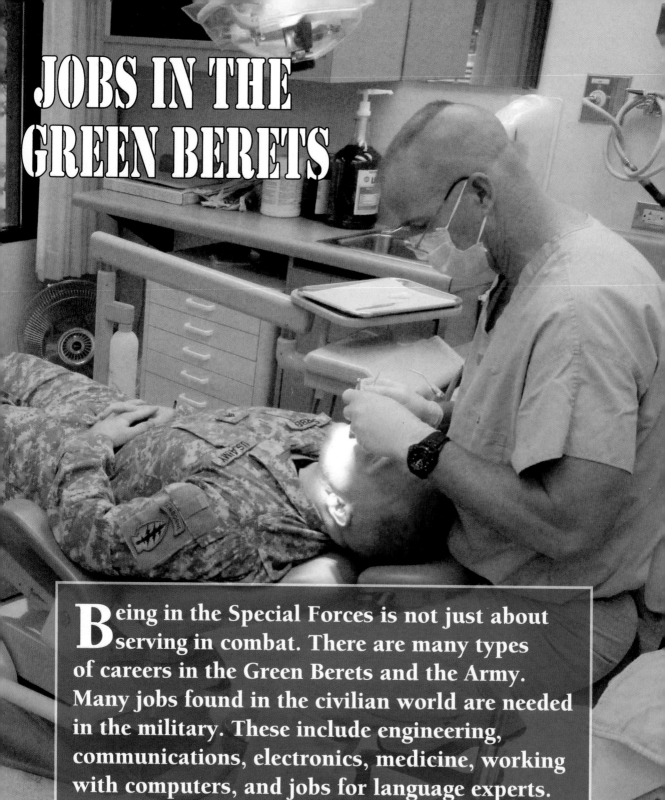

JOBS IN THE GREEN BERETS

Being in the Special Forces is not just about serving in combat. There are many types of careers in the Green Berets and the Army. Many jobs found in the civilian world are needed in the military. These include engineering, communications, electronics, medicine, working with computers, and jobs for language experts. The training and experience gained in the Special Forces can also lead to successful careers in civilian life after military service is completed.

Communications and Technology

These types of jobs involve collecting and studying information, working with computers and electronics, and **military intelligence**. Special Forces communications experts learn to operate a wide variety of communications equipment, from basic radio systems to modern satellite communications.

Linguists and Interpreters

Green Berets spend much of their military career overseas on missions in foreign countries. There are careers for those with detailed knowledge of different cultures and for linguists who can expertly read, write, and speak foreign languages. Jobs involve translating and interpreting languages to help military personnel work more effectively.

Construction and Engineering

Engineers in the Green Berets specialize in many different areas. There are a variety of jobs in construction, such as carpentry, electrical work, and plumbing. Other jobs include designing barriers against the enemy, working with maps and charts, detecting mines and other explosives, and maintaining vehicles and other equipment.

COMMUNITY LIFE

Special Forces personnel often work in secret operations overseas. On bases, however, life in the Special Forces is much like civilian life. Green Berets work regular hours at a job, they spend time with their families, and they fill their free time with hobbies, sports, and other activities. Some Green Berets live in barracks, but others live in houses on or off the base.

Many bases where Green Berets are stationed have all the facilities of most towns and cities. This may include hospitals, schools, day care centers, libraries, sports facilities, and shopping malls. The Special Forces provides a wide variety of programs to improve the quality of life for families living on military bases. These include counseling services, programs to improve on-base education and job opportunities for family members, and programs that help families deal with the stress of having a parent working in a combat area overseas.

★ Many Special Forces personnel are married and have children.

WRITE YOUR STORY

If you apply to join the Green Berets, you will probably need to write an essay about yourself. This is also true when you apply to a college or for a job. Practice telling your story by completing this writing activity.

1 Brainstorming

Start by making notes about your interests. What are your hobbies? Do you like to read? Are you more interested in computers or power tools? Then, organize your ideas into an outline, with a clear beginning, middle, and end.

2 Writing the First Draft

A first draft does not have to be perfect. Try to get the story written. Then, read it to see if it makes sense. It will probably need revision. Even the most famous writers edit their work many times before it is completed.

3 Editing

Go through your story and remove anything that is repeated or not needed. Also, add any missing information that should be included. Be sure the text makes sense and is easy to read.

4 Proofreading

The proofreading is where you check spelling, grammar, and punctuation. You will often find mistakes that you missed during the editing stage. Always look for ways to make your writing the best it can be.

5 Submitting Your Story

When your text is finished, it is time to submit your story, along with any other application materials. A good essay will increase your chances of being accepted, whether it be for a school, a job, or the Green Berets.

TEST YOUR KNOWLEDGE

1  When were the Special Forces founded?

2  How many people currently serve on active duty in the Special Forces?

3  Which Special Forces Group is based at Fort Campbell in Kentucky?

4 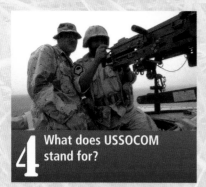 What does USSOCOM stand for?

5  Who called the green beret a "badge of courage"?

6  Where is Special Operations Command Europe located?

7  What is the name of the main pistol used by the Green Berets?

8  What is the Special Forces Qualification Course also known as?

9  What is the Geneva Convention?

10  At what age can a person apply to join the Green Berets?

Answers: 1. 1952 2. About 5,500 3. The 5th Special Forces Group 4. United States Special Operations Command 5. President John F. Kennedy 6. Patch Barracks in Stuttgart, Germany 7. The M9 Beretta 8. Q Course 9. An international treaty that protects soldiers captured during wartime 10. 20 years old

KEY WORDS

civilians: people who are not members of the armed forces

drug trafficking: buying and selling illegal drugs

guerilla warfare: unexpected attacks by small groups of troops within areas occupied by the enemy

hostages: people held prisoner by an enemy until certain conditions are met

magazine: the part of a firearm in which ammunition is stored and fed into the weapon

military intelligence: information about the armed forces of another country

National Guard: the armed forces of individual states that can be called up for active duty when needed

officer: a member of the military who is in a position of authority

reconnaissance: exploration of an area to gather useful information

security clearance: authorization to see information kept secret from the public

semiautomatic: a firing mode in which a gun fires one round, or bullet, and loads a new round each time the trigger is pulled

snipers: highly trained marksmen who shoot at the enemy from concealed positions or long distances without being detected

terrorism: the use of violence or threats to harm or create fear within a country

warheads: the explosive part of a rocket or missile

INDEX

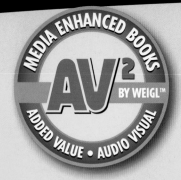

Log on to www.av2books.com

AV² by Weigl brings you media enhanced books that support active learning. Go to www.av2books.com, and enter the special code found on page 2 of this book. You will gain access to enriched and enhanced content that supplements and complements this book. Content includes video, audio, weblinks, quizzes, a slide show, and activities.

AV² Online Navigation

Audio
Listen to sections of the book read aloud.

Video
Watch informative video clips.

Book Pages
AV² pages directly correspond to pages in the book.

Embedded Weblinks
Gain additional information for research.

Key Words
Study vocabulary, and complete a matching word activity.

Try This!
Complete activities and hands-on experiments.

Quizzes
Test your knowledge.

Slide Show
View images and captions, and prepare a presentation.

AV² was built to bridge the gap between print and digital. We encourage you to tell us what you like and what you want to see in the future.

Sign up to be an AV² Ambassador at www.av2books.com/ambassador.

West Fargo Public Library